Introduction ♡

Hello there blessed soul!

Writing down what you're grateful for each day can positively impact the way your body and mind function. It will boost the quality of yoursleep, immunity, and most importantly, it'll make you feel happier. A gratitudejournal is a personal outlet for expressing appreciation for the small blessings in life.

When you journal, it will entirely change your perspective if you spend at least 5 minutes each day focusing on the things you are grateful for. (Once you've gotten into the habit of being grateful and finding joy in everything, you'll want to spread that joy and pay it forward to others!)

More importantly, frequent journaling about the great things in your life will help you prepare and strengthen you to deal with the most chall obstacles in life. Some of the benefits of starting a gratitudenotebook include:

- Gratitude writing might help you feel more balanced and less stressed during the day.
- You may realize that a lot more small, good things are happening – or that the small, good things that were already happening are becoming more apparent.
- Your gratitude may serve as a beacon for good things and good people, generating even more reasons to be thankful.
- Even if it's a minor success, it may make you feel accomplished. Now and then, we all need a win, no matter how big or small.

Starting a new activity or practice can be difficult, especially when it involves a habit that can generate some deep emotions. Don't be surprised if you find it challenging, overwhelming, or intensely emotional at first. Try to lean into the discomfort and stick to your daily gratitude exercise, since greater peace and contentment await on the other side!

Have fun with this gratitude journal! Everyday you can put a gratitude quote of your choice on the section where it says "Quote of the day," so that it can inspire you to be more grateful as a part of your day!

I hope this journal brings you serenity and peacefulness as youwrite down the things you are grateful for! Bring back some joy and happinessin your life by writing in this gratitude journal!

Wishing you the best in all you do,

Mona Liza Santos.

" Enjoy the little things, for one day you may look back and realize they were the big things. "

-- Robert Brault

My Gratitude Journal
(Stay Grateful)
Published by Mona Liza Santos
Copyright © 2022 Mona Liza Santos

For permissions contact:
Authormonaliza@gmail.com
ISBN: 978-1-955560-60-3

This
Gratitude Journal
belongs to:

....

....

....

" We can only be said to be alive in those moments when our hearts are conscious of our treasures."

-- Thornton Wilder

Date: _____   MO TU WE TH FR SA SU

• Quote of the Day

Today I am truly grateful for...

_____

_____

_____

Here's what will make today great...

_____

_____

_____

Some amazing things that happened today...

_____

_____

What could I have done to make today even better?

_____

_____

_____

Date: _____ MO TU WE TH FR SA SU

Plans for Tomorrow...

_____

_____

_____

Thoughts & Reflections for Today

_____
_____
_____
_____
_____
_____
_____
_____
_____
_____
_____
_____
_____
_____
_____
_____
_____
_____
_____
_____
_____
_____

Date: _____   MO TU WE TH FR SA SU

Daily Gratitude Notes:

_____
_____
_____
_____
_____
_____
_____
_____
_____
_____
_____
_____
_____
_____
_____
_____
_____
_____
_____
_____
_____
_____
_____
_____
_____
_____
_____
_____
_____

Date: _____   MO TU WE TH FR SA SU

• Quote of the Day

Today I am truly grateful for...

_____

_____

_____

Here's what will make today great...

_____

_____

_____

Some amazing things that happened today...

_____

_____

What could I have done to make today even better?

_____

_____

_____

Date: _____ MO TU WE TH FR SA SU

Plans for Tomorrow...

_____

_____

_____

Thoughts & Reflections for Today

_____
_____
_____
_____
_____
_____
_____
_____
_____
_____
_____
_____
_____
_____
_____
_____
_____
_____
_____
_____
_____
_____
_____
_____

Date: _____ MO TU WE TH FR SA SU

Daily Gratitude Notes:

_____
_____
_____
_____
_____
_____
_____
_____
_____
_____
_____
_____
_____
_____
_____
_____
_____
_____
_____
_____
_____
_____
_____
_____
_____
_____
_____
_____
_____

Date: _____ MO TU WE TH FR SA SU

• Quote of the Day

Today I am truly grateful for...

_____

_____

_____

Here's what will make today great...

_____

_____

_____

Some amazing things that happened today...

_____

_____

What could I have done to make today even better?

_____

_____

_____

Date: MO TU WE TH FR SA SU

Plans for Tomorrow...

_____

_____

_____

Thoughts & Reflections for Today

_____
_____
_____
_____
_____
_____
_____
_____
_____
_____
_____
_____
_____
_____
_____
_____
_____
_____
_____
_____
_____
_____
_____

Date: MO TU WE TH FR SA SU

Daily Gratitude Notes:

_____

_____

_____

_____

_____

_____

_____

_____

_____

_____

_____

_____

_____

_____

_____

_____

_____

_____

_____

_____

_____

_____

_____

_____

_____

_____

Date: _____ MO TU WE TH FR SA SU

• Quote of the Day

Today I am truly grateful for...

_____

_____

_____

Here's what will make today great...

_____

_____

_____

Some amazing things that happened today...

_____

_____

_____

What could I have done to make today even better?

_____

_____

_____

Date: _____ MO TU WE TH FR SA SU

Plans for Tomorrow...

_____

_____

_____

Thoughts & Reflections for Today

_____
_____
_____
_____
_____
_____
_____
_____
_____
_____
_____
_____
_____
_____
_____
_____
_____
_____
_____
_____
_____
_____
_____

Date: MO TU WE TH FR SA SU

Daily Gratitude Notes:

_____

_____

_____

_____

_____

_____

_____

_____

_____

_____

_____

_____

_____

_____

_____

_____

_____

_____

_____

_____

_____

_____

_____

_____

_____

_____

Date: MO TU WE TH FR SA SU

- Quote of the Day

Today I am truly grateful for...

_____

_____

_____

Here's what will make today great...

_____

_____

_____

Some amazing things that happened today...

_____

_____

_____

What could I have done to make today even better?

_____

_____

_____

Date: _____ MO TU WE TH FR SA SU

Plans for Tomorrow...

_____

_____

_____

Thoughts & Reflections for Today

_____
_____
_____
_____
_____
_____
_____
_____
_____
_____
_____
_____
_____
_____
_____
_____
_____
_____
_____
_____
_____
_____

Date: MO TU WE TH FR SA SU

Daily Gratitude Notes:

_____
_____
_____
_____
_____
_____
_____
_____
_____
_____
_____
_____
_____
_____
_____
_____
_____
_____
_____
_____
_____
_____
_____
_____
_____
_____
_____
_____

Date: _____   MO TU WE TH FR SA SU

• Quote of the Day

Today I am truly grateful for...

- _____

- _____

- _____

Here's what will make today great...

- _____

- _____

- _____

Some amazing things that happened today...

- _____

- _____

- _____

What could I have done to make today even better?

- _____

- _____

- _____

Date: _____   MO TU WE TH FR SA SU

Plans for Tomorrow...

_____

_____

_____

Thoughts & Reflections for Today

_____
_____
_____
_____
_____
_____
_____
_____
_____
_____
_____
_____
_____
_____
_____
_____
_____
_____
_____
_____
_____
_____
_____

Date: _____ MO TU WE TH FR SA SU

Daily Gratitude Notes:

_____
_____
_____
_____
_____
_____
_____
_____
_____
_____
_____
_____
_____
_____
_____
_____
_____
_____
_____
_____
_____
_____
_____
_____
_____
_____
_____
_____

Date: _____   MO TU WE TH FR SA SU

- Quote of the Day

Today I am truly grateful for...

_____

_____

_____

Here's what will make today great...

_____

_____

_____

Some amazing things that happened today...

_____

_____

_____

What could I have done to make today even better?

_____

_____

_____

Date: _____   MO TU WE TH FR SA SU

Plans for Tomorrow...

_____

_____

_____

Thoughts & Reflections for Today

_____

_____

_____

_____

_____

_____

_____

_____

_____

_____

_____

_____

_____

_____

_____

_____

_____

_____

_____

_____

Date: _____   MO TU WE TH FR SA SU

Daily Gratitude Notes:

_____
_____
_____
_____
_____
_____
_____
_____
_____
_____
_____
_____
_____
_____
_____
_____
_____
_____
_____
_____
_____
_____
_____
_____
_____
_____
_____
_____

Date: _____ MO TU WE TH FR SA SU

• Quote of the Day

Today I am truly grateful for...

_____

_____

_____

Here's what will make today great...

_____

_____

_____

Some amazing things that happened today...

_____

_____

_____

What could I have done to make today even better?

_____

_____

_____

Date: _____ MO TU WE TH FR SA SU

Plans for Tomorrow...

_____

_____

_____

Thoughts & Reflections for Today

_____

_____

_____

_____

_____

_____

_____

_____

_____

_____

_____

_____

_____

_____

_____

_____

_____

_____

_____

_____

Date: _____ MO TU WE TH FR SA SU

Daily Gratitude Notes:

_____

_____

_____

_____

_____

_____

_____

_____

_____

_____

_____

_____

_____

_____

_____

_____

_____

_____

_____

_____

_____

_____

_____

_____

_____

_____

Date: _____   MO TU WE TH FR SA SU

- Quote of the Day

Today I am truly grateful for...

_____
_____
_____

Here's what will make today great...

_____
_____
_____

Some amazing things that happened today...

_____
_____
_____

What could I have done to make today even better?

_____
_____
_____

Date: _____ MO TU WE TH FR SA SU

Plans for Tomorrow...

_____

_____

_____

Thoughts & Reflections for Today

_____
_____
_____
_____
_____
_____
_____
_____
_____
_____
_____
_____
_____
_____
_____
_____
_____
_____
_____
_____
_____
_____
_____

Date: MO TU WE TH FR SA SU

Daily Gratitude Notes:

Date: _____   MO TU WE TH FR SA SU

• Quote of the Day

Today I am truly grateful for...

_____

_____

_____

Here's what will make today great...

_____

_____

_____

Some amazing things that happened today...

_____

_____

What could I have done to make today even better?

_____

_____

_____

Date: MO TU WE TH FR SA SU

Plans for Tomorrow...

_____

_____

_____

Thoughts & Reflections for Today

_____
_____
_____
_____
_____
_____
_____
_____
_____
_____
_____
_____
_____
_____
_____
_____
_____
_____
_____
_____
_____

Date: MO TU WE TH FR SA SU

Daily Gratitude Notes:

Date: _____   MO TU WE TH FR SA SU

• Quote of the Day

Today I am truly grateful for...

_____

_____

_____

Here's what will make today great...

_____

_____

_____

Some amazing things that happened today...

_____

_____

_____

What could I have done to make today even better?

_____

_____

_____

Date: _____   MO TU WE TH FR SA SU

Plans for Tomorrow...

_____

_____

_____

Thoughts & Reflections for Today

_____
_____
_____
_____
_____
_____
_____
_____
_____
_____
_____
_____
_____
_____
_____
_____
_____
_____
_____
_____
_____
_____
_____
_____

Date: MO TU WE TH FR SA SU

Daily Gratitude Notes:

Date: _____   MO TU WE TH FR SA SU

• Quote of the Day

Today I am truly grateful for...

_____
_____
_____

Here's what will make today great...

_____
_____
_____

Some amazing things that happened today...

_____
_____
_____

What could I have done to make today even better?

_____
_____
_____

Date: _____ MO TU WE TH FR SA SU

Plans for Tomorrow...

_____

_____

_____

Thoughts & Reflections for Today

_____
_____
_____
_____
_____
_____
_____
_____
_____
_____
_____
_____
_____
_____
_____
_____
_____
_____
_____
_____
_____
_____

Date: MO TU WE TH FR SA SU

Daily Gratitude Notes:

_____
_____
_____
_____
_____
_____
_____
_____
_____
_____
_____
_____
_____
_____
_____
_____
_____
_____
_____
_____
_____
_____
_____
_____
_____
_____
_____
_____
_____

Date: MO TU WE TH FR SA SU

• Quote of the Day

Today I am truly grateful for...

_____

_____

_____

Here's what will make today great...

_____

_____

_____

Some amazing things that happened today...

_____

_____

_____

What could I have done to make today even better?

_____

_____

_____

Date: _____ MO TU WE TH FR SA SU

Plans for Tomorrow...

_____

_____

_____

Thoughts & Reflections for Today

_____
_____
_____
_____
_____
_____
_____
_____
_____
_____
_____
_____
_____
_____
_____
_____
_____
_____
_____
_____
_____
_____

Date: MO TU WE TH FR SA SU

Daily Gratitude Notes:

Date: _____   MO TU WE TH FR SA SU

• Quote of the Day

Today I am truly grateful for...

_____

_____

_____

Here's what will make today great...

_____

_____

_____

Some amazing things that happened today...

_____

_____

_____

What could I have done to make today even better?

_____

_____

_____

Date: _____ MO TU WE TH FR SA SU

Plans for Tomorrow...

_____

_____

_____

Thoughts & Reflections for Today

_____
_____
_____
_____
_____
_____
_____
_____
_____
_____
_____
_____
_____
_____
_____
_____
_____
_____
_____
_____
_____
_____

Date: _____ MO TU WE TH FR SA SU

Daily Gratitude Notes:

_____

_____

_____

_____

_____

_____

_____

_____

_____

_____

_____

_____

_____

_____

_____

_____

_____

_____

_____

_____

_____

_____

_____

_____

_____

_____

_____

_____

_____

_____

Date: _____ MO TU WE TH FR SA SU

• Quote of the Day

Today I am truly grateful for...

_____
_____
_____

Here's what will make today great...

_____
_____
_____

Some amazing things that happened today...

_____
_____
_____

What could I have done to make today even better?

_____
_____
_____

Date: _____ MO TU WE TH FR SA SU

Plans for Tomorrow...

_____

_____

_____

Thoughts & Reflections for Today

_____
_____
_____
_____
_____
_____
_____
_____
_____
_____
_____
_____
_____
_____
_____
_____
_____
_____
_____

Date: MO TU WE TH FR SA SU

Daily Gratitude Notes:

_____
_____
_____
_____
_____
_____
_____
_____
_____
_____
_____
_____
_____
_____
_____
_____
_____
_____
_____
_____
_____
_____
_____
_____
_____
_____
_____

Date: _____ MO TU WE TH FR SA SU

- Quote of the Day

Today I am truly grateful for...

_____
_____
_____

Here's what will make today great...

_____
_____
_____

Some amazing things that happened today...

_____
_____
_____

What could I have done to make today even better?

_____
_____
_____

Date: _____ MO TU WE TH FR SA SU

Plans for Tomorrow...

_____

_____

_____

Thoughts & Reflections for Today

_____
_____
_____
_____
_____
_____
_____
_____
_____
_____
_____
_____
_____
_____
_____
_____
_____
_____
_____
_____
_____
_____

Date: _____ MO TU WE TH FR SA SU

Daily Gratitude Notes:

_____

_____

_____

_____

_____

_____

_____

_____

_____

_____

_____

_____

_____

_____

_____

_____

_____

_____

_____

_____

_____

_____

_____

_____

_____

_____

_____

_____

Date: _____   MO TU WE TH FR SA SU

- Quote of the Day

Today I am truly grateful for...

_____

_____

_____

Here's what will make today great...

_____

_____

_____

Some amazing things that happened today...

_____

_____

_____

What could I have done to make today even better?

_____

_____

_____

Date: _____ MO TU WE TH FR SA SU

Plans for Tomorrow...

_____

_____

_____

Thoughts & Reflections for Today

_____
_____
_____
_____
_____
_____
_____
_____
_____
_____
_____
_____
_____
_____
_____
_____
_____
_____
_____
_____
_____

Date: _____ MO TU WE TH FR SA SU

Daily Gratitude Notes:

_____
_____
_____
_____
_____
_____
_____
_____
_____
_____
_____
_____
_____
_____
_____
_____
_____
_____
_____
_____
_____
_____
_____
_____
_____
_____
_____

Date: _____   MO TU WE TH FR SA SU

• Quote of the Day

Today I am truly grateful for...

_____

_____

_____

Here's what will make today great...

_____

_____

_____

Some amazing things that happened today...

_____

_____

_____

What could I have done to make today even better?

_____

_____

_____

Date: _____ MO TU WE TH FR SA SU

Plans for Tomorrow...

_____

_____

_____

Thoughts & Reflections for Today

_____
_____
_____
_____
_____
_____
_____
_____
_____
_____
_____
_____
_____
_____
_____
_____
_____
_____
_____
_____
_____
_____

Date: _____   MO TU WE TH FR SA SU

Daily Gratitude Notes:

_____
_____
_____
_____
_____
_____
_____
_____
_____
_____
_____
_____
_____
_____
_____
_____
_____
_____
_____
_____
_____
_____
_____
_____
_____
_____
_____
_____
_____

Date: MO TU WE TH FR SA SU

- Quote of the Day

Today I am truly grateful for...

_____
_____
_____

Here's what will make today great...

_____
_____
_____

Some amazing things that happened today...

_____
_____
_____

What could I have done to make today even better?

_____
_____
_____

Date: _____ MO TU WE TH FR SA SU

Plans for Tomorrow...

_____

_____

_____

Thoughts & Reflections for Today

_____
_____
_____
_____
_____
_____
_____
_____
_____
_____
_____
_____
_____
_____
_____
_____
_____
_____
_____
_____
_____
_____
_____

Date: MO TU WE TH FR SA SU

Daily Gratitude Notes:

_____

_____

_____

_____

_____

_____

_____

_____

_____

_____

_____

_____

_____

_____

_____

_____

_____

_____

_____

_____

_____

_____

_____

_____

_____

_____

Date: _____ MO TU WE TH FR SA SU

- Quote of the Day

Today I am truly grateful for...

_____

_____

_____

Here's what will make today great...

_____

_____

_____

Some amazing things that happened today...

_____

_____

_____

What could I have done to make today even better?

_____

_____

_____

Date: _____ MO TU WE TH FR SA SU

Plans for Tomorrow...

_____

_____

_____

Thoughts & Reflections for Today

_____
_____
_____
_____
_____
_____
_____
_____
_____
_____
_____
_____
_____
_____
_____
_____
_____
_____
_____
_____
_____
_____
_____

Date: _____   MO TU WE TH FR SA SU

Daily Gratitude Notes:

_____
_____
_____
_____
_____
_____
_____
_____
_____
_____
_____
_____
_____
_____
_____
_____
_____
_____
_____
_____
_____
_____
_____
_____
_____
_____
_____
_____
_____

Date: MO TU WE TH FR SA SU

- Quote of the Day

Today I am truly grateful for...

_____

_____

Here's what will make today great...

_____

_____

Some amazing things that happened today...

_____

_____

What could I have done to make today even better?

_____

_____

Date: MO TU WE TH FR SA SU

Plans for Tomorrow...

_____

_____

_____

Thoughts & Reflections for Today

_____
_____
_____
_____
_____
_____
_____
_____
_____
_____
_____
_____
_____
_____
_____
_____
_____
_____
_____
_____
_____
_____
_____
_____
_____
_____

Date: MO TU WE TH FR SA SU

Daily Gratitude Notes:

Date: MO TU WE TH FR SA SU

• Quote of the Day

Today I am truly grateful for...

_____

_____

_____

Here's what will make today great...

_____

_____

_____

Some amazing things that happened today...

_____

_____

_____

What could I have done to make today even better?

_____

_____

_____

Date: _____ MO TU WE TH FR SA SU

Plans for Tomorrow...

_____

_____

_____

Thoughts & Reflections for Today

_____
_____
_____
_____
_____
_____
_____
_____
_____
_____
_____
_____
_____
_____
_____
_____
_____
_____
_____
_____
_____
_____

Date: MO TU WE TH FR SA SU

Daily Gratitude Notes:

_____
_____
_____
_____
_____
_____
_____
_____
_____
_____
_____
_____
_____
_____
_____
_____
_____
_____
_____
_____
_____
_____
_____
_____
_____
_____

Date: _____ MO TU WE TH FR SA SU

• Quote of the Day

Today I am truly grateful for...

_____

_____

_____

Here's what will make today great...

_____

_____

_____

Some amazing things that happened today...

_____

_____

_____

What could I have done to make today even better?

_____

_____

_____

Date: MO TU WE TH FR SA SU

Plans for Tomorrow...

_____

_____

_____

Thoughts & Reflections for Today

_____
_____
_____
_____
_____
_____
_____
_____
_____
_____
_____
_____
_____
_____
_____
_____
_____
_____
_____
_____
_____
_____
_____

Date: MO TU WE TH FR SA SU

Daily Gratitude Notes:

Date: _____   MO TU WE TH FR SA SU

- Quote of the Day

Today I am truly grateful for...

_____

_____

_____

Here's what will make today great...

_____

_____

_____

Some amazing things that happened today...

_____

_____

_____

What could I have done to make today even better?

_____

_____

_____

Date: _____ MO TU WE TH FR SA SU

Plans for Tomorrow...

_____

_____

_____

Thoughts & Reflections for Today

_____
_____
_____
_____
_____
_____
_____
_____
_____
_____
_____
_____
_____
_____
_____
_____
_____
_____
_____
_____
_____
_____

Date: _____ MO TU WE TH FR SA SU

Daily Gratitude Notes:

_____
_____
_____
_____
_____
_____
_____
_____
_____
_____
_____
_____
_____
_____
_____
_____
_____
_____
_____
_____
_____
_____
_____
_____
_____
_____
_____
_____

Date: _____ MO TU WE TH FR SA SU

- Quote of the Day

Today I am truly grateful for...

_____

_____

_____

Here's what will make today great...

_____

_____

_____

Some amazing things that happened today...

_____

_____

_____

What could I have done to make today even better?

_____

_____

_____

Date: _____ MO TU WE TH FR SA SU

Plans for Tomorrow...

_____

_____

_____

Thoughts & Reflections for Today

_____

_____

_____

_____

_____

_____

_____

_____

_____

_____

_____

_____

_____

_____

_____

_____

_____

_____

_____

_____

_____

Date: MO TU WE TH FR SA SU

Daily Gratitude Notes:

_____
_____
_____
_____
_____
_____
_____
_____
_____
_____
_____
_____
_____
_____
_____
_____
_____
_____
_____
_____
_____
_____
_____
_____
_____
_____
_____

Date: _____ MO TU WE TH FR SA SU

- Quote of the Day

Today I am truly grateful for...

_____

_____

_____

Here's what will make today great...

_____

_____

_____

Some amazing things that happened today...

_____

_____

_____

What could I have done to make today even better?

_____

_____

_____

Date: _____ MO TU WE TH FR SA SU

Plans for Tomorrow...

_____

_____

_____

Thoughts & Reflections for Today

_____
_____
_____
_____
_____
_____
_____
_____
_____
_____
_____
_____
_____
_____
_____
_____
_____
_____
_____
_____
_____
_____
_____
_____
_____

Date: _____ MO TU WE TH FR SA SU

Daily Gratitude Notes:

_____
_____
_____
_____
_____
_____
_____
_____
_____
_____
_____
_____
_____
_____
_____
_____
_____
_____
_____
_____
_____
_____
_____
_____
_____
_____
_____
_____

Date: MO TU WE TH FR SA SU

• Quote of the Day

Today I am truly grateful for...

_____
_____
_____

Here's what will make today great...

_____
_____
_____

Some amazing things that happened today...

_____
_____

What could I have done to make today even better?

_____
_____
_____

Date: _____ MO TU WE TH FR SA SU

Plans for Tomorrow...

_____

_____

_____

Thoughts & Reflections for Today

_____
_____
_____
_____
_____
_____
_____
_____
_____
_____
_____
_____
_____
_____
_____
_____
_____
_____
_____
_____
_____
_____
_____
_____
_____

Date: _____   MO TU WE TH FR SA SU

Daily Gratitude Notes:

_____
_____
_____
_____
_____
_____
_____
_____
_____
_____
_____
_____
_____
_____
_____
_____
_____
_____
_____
_____
_____
_____
_____
_____
_____
_____

Date: MO TU WE TH FR SA SU

- Quote of the Day

Today I am truly grateful for...

_____

_____

_____

Here's what will make today great...

_____

_____

_____

Some amazing things that happened today...

_____

_____

_____

What could I have done to make today even better?

_____

_____

_____

Date: _____   MO   TU   WE   TH   FR   SA   SU

Plans for Tomorrow...

_____

_____

_____

Thoughts & Reflections for Today

_____
_____
_____
_____
_____
_____
_____
_____
_____
_____
_____
_____
_____
_____
_____
_____
_____
_____
_____
_____
_____
_____

Date: _____ MO TU WE TH FR SA SU

Daily Gratitude Notes:

_____

_____

_____

_____

_____

_____

_____

_____

_____

_____

_____

_____

_____

_____

_____

_____

_____

_____

_____

_____

_____

_____

_____

_____

_____

_____

_____

Date: MO   TU   WE   TH   FR   SA   SU

- Quote of the Day

Today I am truly grateful for...

_____

_____

_____

Here's what will make today great...

_____

_____

_____

Some amazing things that happened today...

_____

_____

_____

What could I have done to make today even better?

_____

_____

_____

Date: _____ MO TU WE TH FR SA SU

Plans for Tomorrow...

_____

_____

_____

Thoughts & Reflections for Today

_____
_____
_____
_____
_____
_____
_____
_____
_____
_____
_____
_____
_____
_____
_____
_____
_____
_____
_____
_____
_____

Date: _____   MO TU WE TH FR SA SU

Daily Gratitude Notes:

_____
_____
_____
_____
_____
_____
_____
_____
_____
_____
_____
_____
_____
_____
_____
_____
_____
_____
_____
_____
_____
_____
_____
_____
_____
_____
_____

Date: _____   MO TU WE TH FR SA SU

• Quote of the Day

Today I am truly grateful for...

_____

_____

_____

Here's what will make today great...

_____

_____

_____

Some amazing things that happened today...

_____

_____

_____

What could I have done to make today even better?

_____

_____

_____

Date: _____ MO TU WE TH FR SA SU

Plans for Tomorrow...

_____

_____

_____

Thoughts & Reflections for Today

_____
_____
_____
_____
_____
_____
_____
_____
_____
_____
_____
_____
_____
_____
_____
_____
_____
_____
_____
_____
_____
_____

Date: _____ MO TU WE TH FR SA SU

Daily Gratitude Notes:

_____

_____

_____

_____

_____

_____

_____

_____

_____

_____

_____

_____

_____

_____

_____

_____

_____

_____

_____

_____

_____

_____

_____

_____

_____

_____

_____

_____

_____

Date: _____   MO TU WE TH FR SA SU

• Quote of the Day

Today I am truly grateful for...

_____

_____

_____

Here's what will make today great...

_____

_____

_____

Some amazing things that happened today...

_____

_____

_____

What could I have done to make today even better?

_____

_____

_____

Date: _____ MO TU WE TH FR SA SU

Plans for Tomorrow...

_____

_____

_____

Thoughts & Reflections for Today

_____

_____

_____

_____

_____

_____

_____

_____

_____

_____

_____

_____

_____

_____

_____

_____

_____

_____

_____

_____

_____

Date: MO TU WE TH FR SA SU

Daily Gratitude Notes:

Date: _____ MO TU WE TH FR SA SU

• Quote of the Day

Today I am truly grateful for...

_____

_____

_____

Here's what will make today great...

_____

_____

_____

Some amazing things that happened today...

_____

_____

What could I have done to make today even better?

_____

_____

_____

Date: _____ MO TU WE TH FR SA SU

Plans for Tomorrow...

_____

_____

_____

Thoughts & Reflections for Today

_____
_____
_____
_____
_____
_____
_____
_____
_____
_____
_____
_____
_____
_____
_____
_____
_____
_____
_____
_____
_____
_____

Date: _____ MO TU WE TH FR SA SU

Daily Gratitude Notes:

_____

_____

_____

_____

_____

_____

_____

_____

_____

_____

_____

_____

_____

_____

_____

_____

_____

_____

_____

_____

_____

_____

_____

Date: MO TU WE TH FR SA SU

- Quote of the Day

Today I am truly grateful for...

_____

_____

_____

Here's what will make today great...

_____

_____

_____

Some amazing things that happened today...

_____

_____

_____

What could I have done to make today even better?

_____

_____

_____

Date: _____ MO TU WE TH FR SA SU

Plans for Tomorrow...

_____

_____

_____

Thoughts & Reflections for Today

_____
_____
_____
_____
_____
_____
_____
_____
_____
_____
_____
_____
_____
_____
_____
_____
_____
_____
_____
_____
_____

Date: MO TU WE TH FR SA SU

Daily Gratitude Notes:

Date: _____   MO TU WE TH FR SA SU

- Quote of the Day

Today I am truly grateful for...

_____

_____

_____

Here's what will make today great...

_____

_____

_____

Some amazing things that happened today...

_____

_____

_____

What could I have done to make today even better?

_____

_____

_____

Date: _____   MO TU WE TH FR SA SU

Plans for Tomorrow...

_____

_____

_____

Thoughts & Reflections for Today

_____

_____

_____

_____

_____

_____

_____

_____

_____

_____

_____

_____

_____

_____

_____

_____

_____

_____

Date: _____ MO TU WE TH FR SA SU

Daily Gratitude Notes:

_____
_____
_____
_____
_____
_____
_____
_____
_____
_____
_____
_____
_____
_____
_____
_____
_____
_____
_____
_____
_____
_____
_____
_____
_____
_____
_____

Date: _____   MO TU WE TH FR SA SU

• Quote of the Day

Today I am truly grateful for...

_____

_____

_____

Here's what will make today great...

_____

_____

_____

Some amazing things that happened today...

_____

_____

_____

What could I have done to make today even better?

_____

_____

_____

Date: _____ MO TU WE TH FR SA SU

Plans for Tomorrow...

_____

_____

_____

Thoughts & Reflections for Today

_____

_____

_____

_____

_____

_____

_____

_____

_____

_____

_____

_____

_____

_____

_____

_____

_____

_____

_____

_____

Date: MO TU WE TH FR SA SU

Daily Gratitude Notes:

Date: _____ MO TU WE TH FR SA SU

- Quote of the Day

Today I am truly grateful for...

_____

_____

_____

Here's what will make today great...

_____

_____

_____

Some amazing things that happened today...

_____

_____

What could I have done to make today even better?

_____

_____

_____

Date: _____   MO TU WE TH FR SA SU

Plans for Tomorrow...

_____

_____

_____

Thoughts & Reflections for Today

_____
_____
_____
_____
_____
_____
_____
_____
_____
_____
_____
_____
_____
_____
_____
_____
_____
_____
_____
_____
_____
_____

Date: **MO TU WE TH FR SA SU**

Daily Gratitude Notes:

_____

_____

_____

_____

_____

_____

_____

_____

_____

_____

_____

_____

_____

_____

_____

_____

_____

_____

_____

_____

_____

_____

_____

_____

_____

_____

_____

_____

_____

_____

Date: MO TU WE TH FR SA SU

- Quote of the Day

Today I am truly grateful for...

_____

_____

_____

Here's what will make today great...

_____

_____

_____

Some amazing things that happened today...

_____

_____

_____

What could I have done to make today even better?

_____

_____

_____

Date: _____   MO TU WE TH FR SA SU

Plans for Tomorrow...

_____

_____

_____

Thoughts & Reflections for Today

_____
_____
_____
_____
_____
_____
_____
_____
_____
_____
_____
_____
_____
_____
_____
_____
_____
_____
_____
_____
_____
_____

Date: MO TU WE TH FR SA SU

Daily Gratitude Notes:

_____
_____
_____
_____
_____
_____
_____
_____
_____
_____
_____
_____
_____
_____
_____
_____
_____
_____
_____
_____
_____
_____
_____
_____
_____

Date: _____ MO TU WE TH FR SA SU

- Quote of the Day

Today I am truly grateful for...

_____

_____

_____

Here's what will make today great...

_____

_____

_____

Some amazing things that happened today...

_____

_____

_____

What could I have done to make today even better?

_____

_____

_____

Date: MO TU WE TH FR SA SU

Plans for Tomorrow...

_____

_____

_____

Thoughts & Reflections for Today

_____
_____
_____
_____
_____
_____
_____
_____
_____
_____
_____
_____
_____
_____
_____
_____
_____
_____
_____
_____
_____
_____
_____
_____

Date: MO TU WE TH FR SA SU

Daily Gratitude Notes:

_____
_____
_____
_____
_____
_____
_____
_____
_____
_____
_____
_____
_____
_____
_____
_____
_____
_____
_____
_____
_____
_____
_____
_____
_____
_____
_____
_____

Date: MO   TU   WE   TH   FR   SA   SU

- Quote of the Day

Today I am truly grateful for...

_____

_____

_____

Here's what will make today great...

_____

_____

_____

Some amazing things that happened today...

_____

_____

_____

What could I have done to make today even better?

_____

_____

_____

Date: MO TU WE TH FR SA SU

Plans for Tomorrow...

_____

_____

_____

Thoughts & Reflections for Today

_____
_____
_____
_____
_____
_____
_____
_____
_____
_____
_____
_____
_____
_____
_____
_____
_____
_____
_____
_____
_____
_____
_____
_____

Date: _____ MO TU WE TH FR SA SU

Daily Gratitude Notes:

_____
_____
_____
_____
_____
_____
_____
_____
_____
_____
_____
_____
_____
_____
_____
_____
_____
_____
_____
_____
_____
_____
_____
_____
_____
_____

Date: _____   MO TU WE TH FR SA SU

• Quote of the Day

Today I am truly grateful for...

_____

_____

_____

Here's what will make today great...

_____

_____

_____

Some amazing things that happened today...

_____

_____

_____

What could I have done to make today even better?

_____

_____

_____

Date: _____ MO TU WE TH FR SA SU

Plans for Tomorrow...

_____

_____

_____

Thoughts & Reflections for Today

_____
_____
_____
_____
_____
_____
_____
_____
_____
_____
_____
_____
_____
_____
_____
_____
_____
_____
_____
_____
_____

Date: MO TU WE TH FR SA SU

Daily Gratitude Notes:

_____

_____

_____

_____

_____

_____

_____

_____

_____

_____

_____

_____

_____

_____

_____

_____

_____

_____

_____

_____

_____

_____

_____

_____

_____

Date: _____ MO TU WE TH FR SA SU

• Quote of the Day

Today I am truly grateful for...

_____

_____

_____

Here's what will make today great...

_____

_____

_____

Some amazing things that happened today...

_____

_____

_____

What could I have done to make today even better?

_____

_____

_____

Date: _____   MO TU WE TH FR SA SU

Plans for Tomorrow...

_____

_____

_____

Thoughts & Reflections for Today

_____
_____
_____
_____
_____
_____
_____
_____
_____
_____
_____
_____
_____
_____
_____
_____
_____
_____
_____
_____
_____
_____
_____

Date: MO TU WE TH FR SA SU

Daily Gratitude Notes:

_____
_____
_____
_____
_____
_____
_____
_____
_____
_____
_____
_____
_____
_____
_____
_____
_____
_____
_____
_____
_____
_____
_____
_____
_____

Date: _____ MO TU WE TH FR SA SU

• Quote of the Day

Today I am truly grateful for...

|——|

|——|

|——|

Here's what will make today great...

|——|

|——|

|——|

Some amazing things that happened today...

|——|

|——|

|——|

What could I have done to make today even better?

|——|

|——|

|——|

Date: _____ MO TU WE TH FR SA SU

Plans for Tomorrow...

_____

_____

_____

Thoughts & Reflections for Today

_____
_____
_____
_____
_____
_____
_____
_____
_____
_____
_____
_____
_____
_____
_____
_____
_____
_____
_____
_____
_____
_____

Date: MO TU WE TH FR SA SU

Daily Gratitude Notes:

Date: _____   MO TU WE TH FR SA SU

• Quote of the Day

Today I am truly grateful for...

_____

_____

_____

Here's what will make today great...

_____

_____

_____

Some amazing things that happened today...

_____

_____

_____

What could I have done to make today even better?

_____

_____

_____

Date: _____ MO TU WE TH FR SA SU

Plans for Tomorrow...

_____

_____

_____

Thoughts & Reflections for Today

_____
_____
_____
_____
_____
_____
_____
_____
_____
_____
_____
_____
_____
_____
_____
_____
_____
_____
_____
_____
_____
_____

Date: _____ MO TU WE TH FR SA SU

Daily Gratitude Notes:

_____
_____
_____
_____
_____
_____
_____
_____
_____
_____
_____
_____
_____
_____
_____
_____
_____
_____
_____
_____
_____
_____
_____
_____
_____

Date: _____ MO TU WE TH FR SA SU

- Quote of the Day

Today I am truly grateful for...

_____

_____

_____

Here's what will make today great...

_____

_____

_____

Some amazing things that happened today...

_____

_____

_____

What could I have done to make today even better?

_____

_____

_____

Date: _____ MO TU WE TH FR SA SU

Plans for Tomorrow...

_____

_____

_____

Thoughts & Reflections for Today

_____
_____
_____
_____
_____
_____
_____
_____
_____
_____
_____
_____
_____
_____
_____
_____
_____
_____
_____
_____
_____
_____

Date: _____ MO TU WE TH FR SA SU

Daily Gratitude Notes:

_____
_____
_____
_____
_____
_____
_____
_____
_____
_____
_____
_____
_____
_____
_____
_____
_____
_____
_____
_____
_____
_____
_____
_____
_____
_____
_____
_____

Date: _____ MO TU WE TH FR SA SU

• Quote of the Day

Today I am truly grateful for...

_____

_____

_____

Here's what will make today great...

_____

_____

_____

Some amazing things that happened today...

_____

_____

_____

What could I have done to make today even better?

_____

_____

_____

Date: _____ MO TU WE TH FR SA SU

Plans for Tomorrow...

_____

_____

_____

Thoughts & Reflections for Today

_____
_____
_____
_____
_____
_____
_____
_____
_____
_____
_____
_____
_____
_____
_____
_____
_____
_____
_____
_____
_____
_____

Date: _____ MO TU WE TH FR SA SU

Daily Gratitude Notes:

_____
_____
_____
_____
_____
_____
_____
_____
_____
_____
_____
_____
_____
_____
_____
_____
_____
_____
_____
_____
_____
_____
_____
_____
_____
_____

Date: _____ MO TU WE TH FR SA SU

- Quote of the Day

Today I am truly grateful for...
_____
_____
_____

Here's what will make today great...
_____
_____
_____

Some amazing things that happened today...
_____
_____
_____

What could I have done to make today even better?
_____
_____
_____

Date: _____ MO TU WE TH FR SA SU

Plans for Tomorrow...

_____

_____

_____

Thoughts & Reflections for Today

_____
_____
_____
_____
_____
_____
_____
_____
_____
_____
_____
_____
_____
_____
_____
_____
_____
_____
_____
_____
_____
_____

Date: _____ MO TU WE TH FR SA SU

Daily Gratitude Notes:

_____
_____
_____
_____
_____
_____
_____
_____
_____
_____
_____
_____
_____
_____
_____
_____
_____
_____
_____
_____
_____
_____
_____
_____
_____
_____
_____
_____

Date: _____   MO TU WE TH FR SA SU

• Quote of the Day

Today I am truly grateful for...

_____

_____

_____

Here's what will make today great...

_____

_____

_____

Some amazing things that happened today...

_____

_____

_____

What could I have done to make today even better?

_____

_____

_____

Date: _____ MO TU WE TH FR SA SU

Plans for Tomorrow...

_____

_____

_____

Thoughts & Reflections for Today

_____
_____
_____
_____
_____
_____
_____
_____
_____
_____
_____
_____
_____
_____
_____
_____
_____
_____
_____
_____
_____
_____
_____

Date: MO TU WE TH FR SA SU

Daily Gratitude Notes:

_____

_____

_____

_____

_____

_____

_____

_____

_____

_____

_____

_____

_____

_____

_____

_____

_____

_____

_____

_____

_____

_____

_____

_____

Date: _____ MO TU WE TH FR SA SU

• Quote of the Day

Today I am truly grateful for...

_____

_____

_____

Here's what will make today great...

_____

_____

_____

Some amazing things that happened today...

_____

_____

_____

What could I have done to make today even better?

_____

_____

_____

Date: _____   MO TU WE TH FR SA SU

Plans for Tomorrow...

_____

_____

_____

Thoughts & Reflections for Today

_____
_____
_____
_____
_____
_____
_____
_____
_____
_____
_____
_____
_____
_____
_____
_____
_____
_____
_____
_____
_____
_____
_____

Date: MO TU WE TH FR SA SU

Daily Gratitude Notes:

Date: _____ MO TU WE TH FR SA SU

• Quote of the Day

Today I am truly grateful for...

_____

_____

_____

Here's what will make today great...

_____

_____

_____

Some amazing things that happened today...

_____

_____

_____

What could I have done to make today even better?

_____

_____

_____

Date: _____ MO TU WE TH FR SA SU

Plans for Tomorrow...

_____

_____

_____

Thoughts & Reflections for Today

_____
_____
_____
_____
_____
_____
_____
_____
_____
_____
_____
_____
_____
_____
_____
_____
_____
_____
_____
_____
_____
_____
_____

Date: _____ MO TU WE TH FR SA SU

Daily Gratitude Notes:

_____
_____
_____
_____
_____
_____
_____
_____
_____
_____
_____
_____
_____
_____
_____
_____
_____
_____
_____
_____
_____
_____
_____
_____
_____
_____
_____

Date: _____ MO TU WE TH FR SA SU

• Quote of the Day

Today I am truly grateful for...

_____
_____
_____

Here's what will make today great...

_____
_____
_____

Some amazing things that happened today...

_____
_____

What could I have done to make today even better?

_____
_____
_____

Date: _____ MO TU WE TH FR SA SU

Plans for Tomorrow...

_____

_____

_____

Thoughts & Reflections for Today

_____

_____

_____

_____

_____

_____

_____

_____

_____

_____

_____

_____

_____

_____

_____

_____

_____

_____

_____

_____

Date: _____ MO TU WE TH FR SA SU

Daily Gratitude Notes:

_____
_____
_____
_____
_____
_____
_____
_____
_____
_____
_____
_____
_____
_____
_____
_____
_____
_____
_____
_____
_____
_____
_____
_____
_____
_____
_____
_____
_____
_____
_____

Date: MO TU WE TH FR SA SU

- Quote of the Day

Today I am truly grateful for...

_____

_____

_____

Here's what will make today great...

_____

_____

_____

Some amazing things that happened today...

_____

_____

_____

What could I have done to make today even better?

_____

_____

_____

Date: _____ MO TU WE TH FR SA SU

Plans for Tomorrow...

_____

_____

_____

Thoughts & Reflections for Today

_____
_____
_____
_____
_____
_____
_____
_____
_____
_____
_____
_____
_____
_____
_____
_____
_____
_____
_____
_____
_____
_____
_____
_____
_____

Date: _____   MO TU WE TH FR SA SU

Daily Gratitude Notes:

_____
_____
_____
_____
_____
_____
_____
_____
_____
_____
_____
_____
_____
_____
_____
_____
_____
_____
_____
_____
_____
_____
_____
_____
_____
_____
_____

Date: _____ MO TU WE TH FR SA SU

- Quote of the Day

Today I am truly grateful for...

_____
_____
_____

Here's what will make today great...

_____
_____
_____

Some amazing things that happened today...

_____
_____
_____

What could I have done to make today even better?

_____
_____
_____

Date: MO TU WE TH FR SA SU

Plans for Tomorrow...

_____

_____

_____

Thoughts & Reflections for Today

_____
_____
_____
_____
_____
_____
_____
_____
_____
_____
_____
_____
_____
_____
_____
_____
_____
_____
_____
_____
_____
_____

Date: MO TU WE TH FR SA SU

Daily Gratitude Notes:

_____
_____
_____
_____
_____
_____
_____
_____
_____
_____
_____
_____
_____
_____
_____
_____
_____
_____
_____
_____
_____
_____
_____
_____
_____
_____
_____
_____
_____
_____
_____
_____

Date: _____   MO TU WE TH FR SA SU

• Quote of the Day

Today I am truly grateful for...

_____

_____

_____

Here's what will make today great...

_____

_____

_____

Some amazing things that happened today...

_____

_____

_____

What could I have done to make today even better?

_____

_____

_____

Date: _____   MO TU WE TH FR SA SU

Plans for Tomorrow...

_____

_____

_____

Thoughts & Reflections for Today

_____
_____
_____
_____
_____
_____
_____
_____
_____
_____
_____
_____
_____
_____
_____
_____
_____
_____
_____
_____
_____
_____
_____

Date: _____   MO TU WE TH FR SA SU

Daily Gratitude Notes:

_____
_____
_____
_____
_____
_____
_____
_____
_____
_____
_____
_____
_____
_____
_____
_____
_____
_____
_____
_____
_____
_____
_____
_____
_____
_____
_____

Date: _____ MO TU WE TH FR SA SU

- Quote of the Day

Today I am truly grateful for...

_____

_____

_____

Here's what will make today great...

_____

_____

_____

Some amazing things that happened today...

_____

_____

_____

What could I have done to make today even better?

_____

_____

_____

Date: _____ MO TU WE TH FR SA SU

Plans for Tomorrow...

_____

_____

_____

Thoughts & Reflections for Today

_____
_____
_____
_____
_____
_____
_____
_____
_____
_____
_____
_____
_____
_____
_____
_____
_____
_____
_____
_____
_____

Date: MO TU WE TH FR SA SU

Daily Gratitude Notes:

_____
_____
_____
_____
_____
_____
_____
_____
_____
_____
_____
_____
_____
_____
_____
_____
_____
_____
_____
_____
_____
_____
_____
_____
_____
_____
_____
_____

Date: _____   MO TU WE TH FR SA SU

• Quote of the Day

Today I am truly grateful for...

_____

_____

_____

Here's what will make today great...

_____

_____

_____

Some amazing things that happened today...

_____

_____

_____

What could I have done to make today even better?

_____

_____

_____

Date: _____ MO TU WE TH FR SA SU

Plans for Tomorrow...

_____

_____

_____

Thoughts & Reflections for Today

_____
_____
_____
_____
_____
_____
_____
_____
_____
_____
_____
_____
_____
_____
_____
_____
_____
_____
_____
_____
_____
_____

Date: _____ MO TU WE TH FR SA SU

Daily Gratitude Notes:

_____

_____

_____

_____

_____

_____

_____

_____

_____

_____

_____

_____

_____

_____

_____

_____

_____

_____

_____

_____

_____

_____

_____

_____

_____

_____

_____

_____

_____

Date: _____ MO TU WE TH FR SA SU

- Quote of the Day

Today I am truly grateful for...

_____

_____

_____

Here's what will make today great...

_____

_____

_____

Some amazing things that happened today...

_____

_____

_____

What could I have done to make today even better?

_____

_____

_____

Date: _____ MO TU WE TH FR SA SU

Plans for Tomorrow...

_____

_____

_____

Thoughts & Reflections for Today

_____
_____
_____
_____
_____
_____
_____
_____
_____
_____
_____
_____
_____
_____
_____
_____
_____
_____
_____
_____
_____
_____
_____

Date: _____   MO TU WE TH FR SA SU

Daily Gratitude Notes:

_____
_____
_____
_____
_____
_____
_____
_____
_____
_____
_____
_____
_____
_____
_____
_____
_____
_____
_____
_____
_____
_____
_____
_____
_____
_____
_____
_____

Date: MO TU WE TH FR SA SU

• Quote of the Day

Today I am truly grateful for...

_____

_____

_____

Here's what will make today great...

_____

_____

_____

Some amazing things that happened today...

_____

_____

_____

What could I have done to make today even better?

_____

_____

_____

Date: MO TU WE TH FR SA SU

Plans for Tomorrow...

_____

_____

_____

Thoughts & Reflections for Today

_____

_____

_____

_____

_____

_____

_____

_____

_____

_____

_____

_____

_____

_____

_____

_____

_____

_____

_____

_____

_____

Date: _____   MO TU WE TH FR SA SU

Daily Gratitude Notes:

_____
_____
_____
_____
_____
_____
_____
_____
_____
_____
_____
_____
_____
_____
_____
_____
_____
_____
_____
_____
_____
_____
_____
_____
_____
_____
_____
_____

Date: _____ MO TU WE TH FR SA SU

- Quote of the Day

Today I am truly grateful for...

_____

_____

_____

Here's what will make today great...

_____

_____

_____

Some amazing things that happened today...

_____

_____

_____

What could I have done to make today even better?

_____

_____

_____

Date: _____ MO TU WE TH FR SA SU

Plans for Tomorrow...

_____

_____

_____

Thoughts & Reflections for Today

_____
_____
_____
_____
_____
_____
_____
_____
_____
_____
_____
_____
_____
_____
_____
_____
_____
_____
_____
_____

Date: MO TU WE TH FR SA SU

Daily Gratitude Notes:

_____

_____
_____
_____
_____
_____
_____
_____
_____
_____
_____
_____
_____
_____
_____
_____
_____
_____
_____
_____
_____
_____
_____
_____
_____
_____
_____

Date: MO TU WE TH FR SA SU

- Quote of the Day

Today I am truly grateful for...

_____

_____

_____

Here's what will make today great...

_____

_____

_____

Some amazing things that happened today...

_____

_____

_____

What could I have done to make today even better?

_____

_____

_____

Date: _____ MO TU WE TH FR SA SU

Plans for Tomorrow...

_____

_____

_____

Thoughts & Reflections for Today

_____
_____
_____
_____
_____
_____
_____
_____
_____
_____
_____
_____
_____
_____
_____
_____
_____
_____
_____
_____
_____
_____
_____

Date: _____   MO TU WE TH FR SA SU

Daily Gratitude Notes:

_____
_____
_____
_____
_____
_____
_____
_____
_____
_____
_____
_____
_____
_____
_____
_____
_____
_____
_____
_____
_____
_____
_____
_____
_____
_____

Date: _____ MO TU WE TH FR SA SU

- Quote of the Day

Today I am truly grateful for...

_____

_____

_____

Here's what will make today great...

_____

_____

_____

Some amazing things that happened today...

_____

_____

_____

What could I have done to make today even better?

_____

_____

_____

Date: _____   MO TU WE TH FR SA SU

Plans for Tomorrow...

_____

_____

_____

Thoughts & Reflections for Today

_____
_____
_____
_____
_____
_____
_____
_____
_____
_____
_____
_____
_____
_____
_____
_____
_____
_____
_____
_____
_____
_____
_____
_____

Date: _____ MO TU WE TH FR SA SU

Daily Gratitude Notes:

_____

_____

_____

_____

_____

_____

_____

_____

_____

_____

_____

_____

_____

_____

_____

_____

_____

_____

_____

_____

_____

_____

_____

_____

_____

_____

_____

_____

If you enjoyed this journal and would like to
purchase more or see other designs,
check out:

https://www.monalizasantos.com/notebooks-journals

Thank you for your support!
Stay awesome and always grateful! ♥

www.ingramcontent.com/pod-product-compliance
Lightning Source LLC
Chambersburg PA
CBHW052113030426
42335CB00025B/2966